THE FUTURE OF UAV CONTROL: FORCE SENSOR-BASED SINGLE-HANDED OPERATION AND BEYOND

MR. SUDHANSHU PRASAD
MR. SOMNATH SATAPATHY
MR. AYES CHINMAY

SHORT DESCRIPTION OF THE BOOK

"The Future of UAV Control: Force Sensor-Based Single-Handed Operation and Beyond" explores the cutting-edge advancements and potential of force sensor-based control systems in unmanned aerial vehicle (UAV) operations. This comprehensive book delves into the fundamentals of UAV control, the integration of force sensors into control interfaces, the design and implementation of single-handed control, performance evaluation metrics, user experience assessment, and the future possibilities of UAV control. Readers will gain insights into the limitations of traditional control interfaces and the motivation behind force sensor-based single-handed operation. The book examines various types of force sensors used in UAV control, their integration into control interfaces, and the advantages they offer. It also delves into human factors considerations, design principles, and ergonomic aspects of single-handed control systems. The book includes comparative analysis between force sensor-based control and traditional control systems, providing a comprehensive understanding of their strengths and limitations. The book also touches on advanced control techniques beyond single-handed operation, including multi-modal interfaces, haptic feedback, augmented reality, voice control, and gesture-based control. "The Future of UAV Control" provides a holistic view of the possibilities and challenges in UAV control, offering valuable insights to researchers, engineers, UAV operators, and anyone interested in the future of drone technology and its control systems.*

First Printing Edition, 2023

ISBN: 979-8850218584

❀❀❀

TABLE OF CONTENTS

ABOUT THE AUTHORS

S udhanshu Prasad has done his 12th from DAV Public school, Bariatu. He is pursuing his B.Tech student in the department of Computer Science and Engineering, ITER, Siksha 'O' Anusandhan (Deemed to be University), Bhubaneswar, Odisha. He has worked on some IOT based projects with Arduino and he has also worked on Ardupilot based autopilot system for Drones and Linux based operating system and single board computers like Raspberry Pi. Also, he has done web development with MERN stack and deployment on AWS. He has worked with 3D printing technology and he has filed 3 patents.

S omnath Satapathy is a B.Tech student of department of Computer Science and Engineering, ITER, Siksha 'O' Anusandhan (Deemed to be University), Bhubaneswar, Odisha. He has worked on some web-based projects namely sunofy: a spotify like music recommendation website built with React using Typescrypt which he has deployed using AWS Amplify. AlsiSaanp: a web-based app which stores the high score of each user in the browser local storage. He also has experience of being a core member of Dr. Braja Vihari Mohanty Memorial Mentally Retarded Benefit Trust (BVMR Trust).

A yes Chinmay received his B. Tech degree in Computer Science and Engineering from TAT Bhubaneswar, Odisha, in 2015. He received his M. Tech degree in Computer Science and Engineering from IIIT Bhubaneswar, Odisha, in 2017. Since 2017, he has been working as a Ph.D. scholar in the department of Computer Science and Engineering, IIIT Bhubaneswar, Odisha. His research interest includes VoWi-Fi, IoT, Li-Fi and WLAN. He is an Assistant Professor in the department of Computer Science and Engineering, ITER, Siksha 'O' Anusandhan (Deemed to be University), Bhubaneswar, Odisha. He has developed Pradhanmantri Awaas Yojana dashboard and Mo Sarkar web application for Government of Odisha. He has published more than 20 research papers in prestigious journals, conferences. He has published 6 international books. He has 3 granted patents and published more than 15 national & international patents.

MR. SUDHANSHU PRASAD

MR. SOMNATH SATAPATHY

MR. AYES CHINMAY

THE FUTURE OF UAV CONTROL: FORCE SENSOR-BASED SINGLE-HANDED OPERATION AND BEYOND

CHAPTER 01

INTRODUCTION

1.1 Background and Significance of UAV Control

Unmanned Aerial Vehicles (UAVs), commonly known as drones, have witnessed remarkable advancements in recent years. These versatile flying machines have revolutionized various industries, including aerial photography, videography, surveillance, search and rescue, agriculture, and delivery services. As the demand for UAVs continues to grow, there is a need for more intuitive and efficient control systems to enhance their usability and performance.

Traditionally, UAV control has been predominantly reliant on handheld remote controllers with joysticks or mobile device-based interfaces. While these control methods have served their purpose, they often present challenges such as steep learning curves, limited dexterity, and complex coordination between hands. As UAVs become more sophisticated and capable, the need for more intuitive and natural control interfaces becomes increasingly evident.

1.2 Evolution of UAV Control Systems

The evolution of UAV control systems has seen significant progress, driven by advancements in technology and user demands. Early UAVs were primarily controlled through manual radio frequency (RF) remote controllers, which required precise manipulation of multiple joysticks. As UAV technology improved, control systems evolved to include mobile apps with touch-based interfaces, enabling more accessible control for casual users.

The introduction of motion-sensing technologies, such as accelerometers and gyroscopes, further expanded the possibilities for controlling UAVs by tilting or shaking the mobile device. However, these methods still relied heavily on manual input and lacked the seamless integration of human touch and force feedback.

1.3 Motivation for Force Sensor-Based Single-Handed Operation

The motivation behind force sensor-based single-handed operation arises from the need for a more natural and intuitive control interface that closely mimics the way humans interact with objects in the physical world. By incorporating force sensors into UAV control systems, users can manipulate the drone's movements through the application of force and pressure, as they would with real-world objects.

Force sensor-based control systems offer several advantages over traditional control methods. They provide a more ergonomic and efficient way of operating UAVs, reducing user fatigue and improving precision. Single-handed operation allows users to free up their other hand for additional tasks or emergency situations. Furthermore, force feedback from the sensors can enhance situational awareness and improve the user's sense of control and immersion.

1.4 Objectives and Structure of the Book

The primary objective of this book is to explore the future of UAV control, with a specific focus on force sensor-based single-handed operation and its potential beyond. It aims to provide readers with a comprehensive understanding of the principles, design considerations, applications, and challenges associated with force sensor-based control systems for UAVs.

The book is organized into several chapters, each focusing on a specific aspect of UAV control. Chapter 2 introduces the fundamentals of UAV control and discusses the limitations of existing control systems. Chapter 3 delves into force sensor technology and its integration into UAV control interfaces. Chapter 4 explores the design and implementation of single-handed control systems, emphasizing human factors and ergonomic considerations. Chapter 5 discusses performance evaluation and user experience metrics for force sensor-based control systems, drawing comparisons with traditional control methods.

The book also includes an appendix with technical specifications and resources related to force sensor technologies, a glossary to define key terms, and an index for easy reference.

In conclusion, this book aims to shed light on the exciting
advancements in UAV control, specifically focusing on force
sensor-based single-handed operation. By exploring the
potentials and challenges of this emerging field, readers will
gain insights into the future of UAV control and its broader
applications beyond force sensor-based interfaces.

CHAPTER 02

FUNDAMENTALS OF UAV CONTROL

2.1 Overview of Traditional UAV Control Interfaces

UAV control interfaces have undergone significant evolution over the years, aiming to provide users with intuitive and efficient control over these unmanned flying machines. Traditional control interfaces have predominantly relied on handheld remote controllers with joysticks or mobile device-based applications.

Handheld remote controllers consist of a transmitter that communicates with the UAV through radio frequency (RF) signals. These controllers typically feature joysticks, switches, and buttons to manipulate the UAV's flight parameters such as throttle, pitch, roll, and yaw. While familiar to experienced users, remote controllers often have steep learning curves and require hand-eye coordination and skill to operate effectively.

Mobile device-based control interfaces leverage the ubiquity of smartphones and tablets to provide an accessible means of controlling UAVs. These interfaces typically involve touchscreen interactions, allowing users to tap and swipe on the device's display to control the UAV's movements. Mobile apps also provide additional features such as live video streaming and waypoint-based navigation.

2.2 Challenges and Limitations of Existing Control Systems

Although traditional control interfaces have facilitated the widespread use of UAVs, they are not without limitations. These limitations have fueled the need for more advanced control systems, such as force sensor-based single-handed operation.

One of the challenges is the steep learning curve associated with traditional control interfaces. Novice users often struggle to grasp the precise manipulation of joysticks or the coordination required to control multiple parameters simultaneously. This barrier to entry restricts the accessibility of UAVs to a broader audience.

Another limitation is the lack of natural and intuitive control. Traditional interfaces require users to translate their intentions into abstract movements on joysticks or touchscreen controls. This disconnects between the physical input and the resulting UAV movement can hinder the user's ability to operate the drone accurately and efficiently.

Furthermore, traditional control interfaces often demand the use of both hands, which limits the user's ability to perform additional tasks simultaneously. This restriction becomes more apparent in scenarios where a user needs to interact with objects or navigate challenging environments while controlling the UAV.

2.3 Introduction to Force Sensor Technology

Force sensor technology has emerged as a promising solution to overcome the limitations of traditional UAV control interfaces. Force sensors are devices that detect and measure the applied force or pressure. By integrating force sensors into UAV control systems, users can manipulate the drone's movements through the application of force and pressure, simulating interactions with physical objects.

Force sensors come in various forms, including strain gauges, capacitive sensors, piezoelectric sensors, and optical sensors. These sensors can be incorporated into different parts of the control interface, such as the handles or grips, to capture the user's applied force accurately.

2.4 Principles of Force-Based Control

Force-based control relies on the principles of haptic feedback and force sensing to enable a more natural and intuitive control interface. The primary principle is that the user applies force or pressure on the control interface, and the force sensors capture and transmit this input to the UAV's control system.

The UAV's control system interprets the force input and translates it into appropriate commands for controlling the drone's flight parameters, such as altitude, orientation, or speed. The control system uses algorithms to convert the force data into meaningful control signals that govern the UAV's movements.

Force-based control systems can also provide haptic feedback to the user. Haptic feedback refers to the tactile sensations or vibrations that users perceive when interacting with force sensor-based interfaces. This feedback enhances the user's situational awareness by providing a sense of touch and physical interaction with the UAV, improving control precision and immersion.

By incorporating force-based control principles, UAV control systems can offer a more ergonomic, intuitive, and immersive user experience. Users can manipulate the drone's movements more naturally, leveraging their tactile senses and physical intuition.

In the next chapter, we will explore in detail the different types of force sensors used in UAV control and how they are integrated into control interfaces. We will also discuss the advantages and potential applications of force sensor-based control systems.

CHAPTER 03

FORCE SENSOR-BASED CONTROL SYSTEMS

3.1 Overview of Force Sensor-Based Control Systems

Force sensor-based control systems represent a paradigm shift in UAV control, offering a more natural and intuitive way of interacting with unmanned aerial vehicles. These systems leverage force sensor technology to capture the user's applied force or pressure and translate it into control commands for the UAV.

Force sensors can be integrated into various components of the control interface, such as handles, grips, or control surfaces. They measure the force exerted by the user and provide real-time feedback to the UAV's control system. This feedback enables precise and responsive control over the drone's movements, enhancing user experience and performance.

3.2 Types of Force Sensors Used in UAV Control

Several types of force sensors are used in force sensor-based control systems for UAVs. These sensors vary in their underlying principles and sensing mechanisms. Some common types of force sensors include:

3.2.1 Strain Gauges:

Strain gauges are sensors that measure the strain or deformation of an object subjected to force. They work on the principle that the electrical resistance of a conductor changes proportionally with the applied force. Strain gauges are often used in the form of flexible or thin-film sensors that can be integrated into the control interface.

3.2.2 Capacitive Sensors:

Capacitive sensors detect changes in capacitance caused by the applied force. They consist of two conductive plates separated by a dielectric material. When force is applied, the distance between the plates changes, altering the capacitance.

Capacitive sensors are sensitive and can provide accurate force measurements.

3.2.3 Piezoelectric Sensors:

Piezoelectric sensors generate an electrical charge when subjected to mechanical stress or pressure. These sensors utilize piezoelectric materials that produce voltage proportional to the applied force. They are highly responsive and can capture rapid force changes effectively.

3.2.4 Optical Sensors:

Optical force sensors use light to measure the displacement caused by the applied force. These sensors employ techniques such as fiber optic interferometry or intensity modulation to detect changes in light patterns. Optical sensors offer high accuracy and can handle both static and dynamic force measurements.

3.3 Integration of Force Sensors into UAV Control Interfaces

Integrating force sensors into UAV control interfaces involves careful design and engineering considerations. The placement and configuration of force sensors play a crucial role in capturing accurate force data and providing a seamless user experience.

Force sensors can be integrated into the handles or grips of handheld controllers, allowing users to apply force directly while holding the device. They can also be embedded within control surfaces, such as buttons, sliders, or touch-sensitive panels, enabling force-based interactions in specific areas of the interface.

The data from force sensors is typically processed and transmitted to the UAV's control system through wired or wireless connections. The control system interprets the force input and generates appropriate control commands to manipulate the drone's flight parameters accordingly.

3.4 Advantages and Potential Applications of Force Sensor-Based Control

Force sensor-based control systems offer numerous advantages over traditional control methods, unlocking new possibilities for UAV control. Some key advantages include:

3.4.1 Intuitive and Natural Interaction:

Force-based control systems allow users to interact with UAVs in a more natural and intuitive manner, leveraging their sense of touch and physical intuition. Users can manipulate the drone's movements by applying force, simulating real-world object interactions.

3.4.2 Ergonomic and Efficient Operation:

Force sensor-based control systems provide ergonomic benefits by reducing user fatigue and strain. Single-handed operation enables users to perform additional tasks or respond to emergency situations more effectively while controlling the UAV.

3.4.3 Enhanced Precision and Immersion:

The integration of force sensors and haptic feedback in control interfaces enhances the user's precision and situational awareness.

Users receive tactile feedback that enhances their sense of control and immersion, improving overall performance.

Force sensor-based control systems have a wide range of potential applications in UAV operations. Some notable applications include:

- Aerial Photography and Videography: Force-based control allows photographers and videographers to precisely control the UAV's positioning, angles, and camera movements, enabling captivating aerial shots.

- Industrial Inspection and Maintenance: Force sensor-based control systems can be used for inspecting infrastructure, such as power lines, pipelines, or bridges. The precise force control enables operators to navigate challenging environments and perform detailed inspections.

- Search and Rescue Operations: UAVs equipped with force sensor-based control systems can aid in search and rescue missions. The intuitive control interface allows operators to maneuver the drone effectively in complex terrains or confined spaces, enhancing search capabilities.

- Military and Defense Applications: Force sensor-based control systems have potential applications in military and defense operations. They can be used for reconnaissance, surveillance, and even weaponized drones, providing more precise control and operational flexibility.

In the next chapter, we will delve into the design and implementation of single-handed control systems, focusing on human factors considerations and ergonomic design principles.

CHAPTER 04

DESIGN AND
IMPLEMENTATION OF
SINGLE-HANDED CONTROL

4.1 Human Factors Considerations in Single-Handed Control Design

Designing single-handed control systems for UAVs requires careful consideration of human factors to ensure optimal user experience and performance. Human factors encompass the physical, cognitive, and ergonomic aspects of human interaction with technology. Here are key considerations:

4.1.1 Ergonomics:

The design should prioritize ergonomics to ensure that the control interface fits comfortably in the user's hand. Factors such as grip size, button placement, and weight distribution should be optimized to reduce fatigue and enhance user control.

4.1.2 Reachability:

The placement of controls and buttons should be within the user's natural reach to minimize the need for hand repositioning or excessive finger movement. This allows for quick and efficient access to essential functions during UAV operation.

4.1.3 Feedback and Awareness:

Providing clear and intuitive feedback to the user is crucial for situational awareness. Visual indicators, haptic feedback, and auditory cues can enhance the user's understanding of the UAV's status, such as battery level, altitude, or flight mode.

4.1.4 Learnability:

Single-handed control systems should be designed with a shallow learning curve to facilitate ease of use for both novice and experienced users. Intuitive control mapping and minimal cognitive load contribute to faster skill acquisition and improved control proficiency.

4.2 Design Principles and Ergonomic Considerations for Single-Handed Control

Design principles play a vital role in creating effective and user-friendly single-handed control systems for UAVs. Here are key design principles and ergonomic considerations:

4.2.1 Form Factor:

The control interface should have an ergonomic shape that fits comfortably in the user's hand, allowing for a secure grip and reducing the risk of accidental drops or slippage during operation. Contoured and textured surfaces can enhance tactile feedback and grip stability.

4.2.2 Button Layout and Accessibility:

The placement and arrangement of buttons, switches, and sliders should be intuitive and accessible within the user's thumb or finger reach. Logical grouping and differentiation through shape, size, or color coding can enhance control efficiency.

4.2.3 Force Sensor Integration:

Force sensors should be integrated into the control interface in a way that allows users to apply force naturally without exerting excessive effort. The force sensors should be strategically placed to capture user input accurately and provide precise control.

4.2.4 Haptic Feedback:

Integrating haptic feedback mechanisms, such as vibration motors or tactile actuators, can provide users with tactile cues and enhance their perception of control. Haptic feedback can indicate button presses, force thresholds, or provide warnings/alerts during operation.

4.2.5 Customizability:

Providing users with the flexibility to customize button assignments, sensitivity settings, or control mappings can accommodate individual preferences and adapt to specific use cases or skill levels. Customizability empowers users to optimize the control system to their unique needs.

4.3 Integration of Force Sensors into Single-Handed Control Interfaces

Integrating force sensors into single-handed control interfaces involves careful engineering and technical considerations. The following steps outline the integration process:

4.3.1 Sensor Selection:

Choosing the appropriate type of force sensor based on factors such as accuracy, response time, and compatibility with the control interface design.

4.3.2 Sensor Placement:

Determining the optimal locations within the control interface to position the force sensors, considering factors such as hand anatomy, natural force application, and ergonomic grip.

4.3.3 Sensor Calibration:

Calibrating the force sensors to ensure accurate and reliable force measurements. Calibration involves establishing the force-to-signal relationship and compensating for any environmental factors that may impact sensor readings.

4.3.4 Signal Processing:

Processing the force sensor data to extract meaningful force values. This involves filtering, amplifying, and converting the analog force signals into digital form suitable for control system interpretation.

4.3.5 Control System Integration:

Integrating the force sensor data into the UAV's control system. This includes mapping the force inputs to appropriate control commands, such as throttle, pitch, roll, and yaw, based on predefined control algorithms.

4.4 Case Studies and Examples of Single-Handed Control Systems

This chapter presents case studies and examples of single-handed control systems implemented in UAV control. These case studies highlight successful designs, user experiences, and the advantages of single-handed control in various applications, such as aerial photography, inspection, and search and rescue.

In the next chapter, we will explore performance evaluation metrics and user experience assessment methodologies for force sensor-based control systems, providing insights into their effectiveness and user satisfaction.

CHAPTER 05

PERFORMANCE EVALUATION AND USER EXPERIENCE

5.1 Metrics for Evaluating the Performance of Force Sensor-Based Control Systems

Evaluating the performance of force sensor-based control systems is essential to assess their effectiveness, usability, and overall performance. Several metrics can be used to evaluate these systems:

5.1.1 Control Accuracy:

Control accuracy measures the precision with which the UAV responds to user input. It can be evaluated by comparing the intended command with the actual movement or position of the drone. Metrics such as error distance, deviation from the target, or positional accuracy can be used to quantify control accuracy.

5.1.2 Responsiveness:

Responsiveness refers to the speed at which the UAV reacts to user commands. It can be measured by analyzing the time delay between the user's input and the corresponding drone action. Lower time delays indicate higher responsiveness.

5.1.3 Efficiency:

Efficiency measures how effectively users can achieve their control objectives using the force sensor-based interface. It can be assessed by evaluating the time required to perform specific tasks or maneuvers compared to traditional control methods. Faster task completion times indicate higher efficiency.

5.1.4 Workload:

Workload assessment determines the cognitive and physical demands placed on users while operating the UAV. Subjective assessments, such as workload rating scales or questionnaires, can provide insights into the perceived workload. Physiological measurements, such as heart rate or eye-tracking, can also be used to quantify workload objectively.

5.2 Experimental Methodologies for Assessing User Experience and Satisfaction

User experience and satisfaction are critical factors in evaluating the usability and acceptability of force sensor-based control systems. Various experimental methodologies can be employed to assess user experience:

5.2.1 Usability Testing:

Usability testing involves conducting controlled experiments where users perform specific tasks using the control interface. Observations, task completion times, errors, and user feedback are collected to assess the system's ease of use, learnability, and efficiency.

5.2.2 User Surveys and Questionnaires:

Surveys and questionnaires provide a structured way to gather user feedback and opinions about their experience with the force sensor-based control system. Questions can cover aspects such as ease of use, intuitiveness, comfort, and overall satisfaction.

5.2.3 Focus Groups and Interviews:

Focus groups and interviews allow for in-depth discussions with users to gain qualitative insights into their experiences, perceptions, and suggestions for improving the control system. These methods can provide rich contextual information and uncover nuanced user perspectives.

5.2.4 Comparative Studies:

Comparative studies involve comparing force sensor-based control systems with traditional control methods, such as joysticks or touch-based interfaces. Users perform tasks using both systems, and their performance, preferences, and subjective feedback are collected for analysis.

5.3 Comparative Analysis of Force Sensor-Based Control versus Traditional Control Systems

A comparative analysis between force sensor-based control systems and traditional control systems can shed light on the advantages and limitations of each approach. Factors to consider in the comparative analysis include:

5.3.1 Learning Curve:

Assessing the ease of learning and skill acquisition for both control methods. Comparing the time required for users to become proficient in each system.

5.3.2 Control Precision:

Evaluating the precision and accuracy of control inputs for both systems. Comparing the ability to perform precise maneuvers or maintain stable flight.

5.3.3 Immersion and Presence:

Analyzing the user's sense of immersion and presence with each control system. Comparing the extent to which users feel connected to the UAV and their environment.

5.3.4 User Preferences and Satisfaction:

Gathering user feedback to determine preferences and satisfaction levels for each control system. Identifying which system users find more intuitive, comfortable, and enjoyable to use.

5.4 Feedback from Users and Operators

Collecting feedback from users and operators who have hands-on experience with force sensor-based control systems is invaluable. Feedback can be gathered through surveys, interviews, or direct observations during real-world operations. This feedback can provide insights into the strengths, weaknesses, and areas of improvement for the control system.

In the next chapter, we will explore advanced control techniques beyond single-handed control, including multi-modal interfaces, haptic feedback, augmented reality, voice control, and gesture-based control, showcasing the future possibilities in UAV control.